Hasty Pudding, Johnnycakes, and Other Good Stuff

Cooking in Colonial America

LORETTA FRANCES ICHORD

illustrated by Jan Davey Ellis

THE MILLBROOK PRESS   BROOKFIELD, CONNECTICUT

*To my loving and supportive daughter, Tina Ichord Johansson,
and all other dedicated teachers.*

LI

I would like to thank the hardworking and dedicated tour guides who took me through
historic Mount Vernon, the home of George Washington, as well as those who took me through
Monticello, the home of Thomas Jefferson. I would also like to thank Dennis Cotner, Team
Leader of Historic Foodways in Colonial Williamsburg, Virginia, for the valuable information he
so kindly provided.

Library of Congress Cataloging-in-Publication Data
Ichord, Loretta Frances.
Hasty pudding, johnnycakes, and other good stuff : cooking in colonial America / by Loretta Frances
Ichord; illustrated by Jan Davey Ellis.
  p.   cm.
Includes bibliographical references.
Summary: Presents colonial food preparation with a look at the influences of available ingredients,
cooking methods, and equipment. Includes recipes and appendix of classroom cooking directions.
ISBN 0-7613-0369-3 (lib. bdg.) — ISBN 0-7613-1297-8 (pbk.)
1. Cookery, American—History—Juvenile literature. 2. United States—History—Colonial period,
ca. 1600–1775—Juvenile literature. 3. Food habits—United States—History—17th century—Juvenile literature. 4. Food habits—United States—History—18th century—Juvenile literature. [1. Cookery, American—History. 2. United States—History—Colonial period, ca. 1600–1775.]
I. Ellis, Jan Davey, ill. II. Title.
TX715.I224 1998
641.5973'09'032—dc2l   97-47094   CIP   AC

Published by The Millbrook Press
2 Old New Milford Road
Brookfield, CT 06804

Printed in the United States of America
(lib. bdg.) 5   4   3   2
(pbk.)   5   4   3   2   1

CONTENTS

INTRODUCTION

Can you think of common everyday foods that Americans eat? Probably tacos, French fries, and pizzas come to mind because they are widely available, inexpensive, and easy to prepare. All of these foods came to America from other countries. Besides eating foreign fast food, Americans often dine out at fine restaurants that serve French or Italian cuisine. There are also Chinese, Japanese, Mexican, and Middle Eastern establishments, among others, that provide an array of tasty choices. But, do we ever say, "Let's go out for American food?"

After all, what is American food? Certainly fried chicken, hamburgers, and chocolate cake to name a few—but these are all relatively modern additions to our cuisine. What is our American culinary heritage? How did cooking begin in America?

The first settlers who came to America in the 1600s would have starved to death if not for the already developed cuisine of the Native Americans. These people showed the colonists how to survive in the wilderness by trapping, fishing, and cultivating corn, a nutritious and easy-to-grow crop. The settlers also learned from the Native Americans how to grow beans and squash among the corn rows. It was from these foods that the beginning of a unique American cuisine developed. From the time the first settlers arrived in 1607 and through the early days of colonization, food was limited and conditions were primitive. But the colonial period lasted until the end of the American Revolution, in 1783, and by that time agriculture had developed and cooking conditions were more sophisticated.

This book is about what foods were available and how they were prepared in the colonial period. There are recipes included that will give you an authentic taste of what you would have been eating if you lived in America between 1607 and 1783. Most of them call for the use of kitchen equipment that will require an adult to work with you. If you would like to share a taste of early America with a larger group as part of a report or class project, directions at the end of the book will tell you how to increase the recipes.

All the recipes have been adapted to modern ingredients and cooking appliances without loss of authenticity, but each recipe includes notes on how a colonial cook would have prepared the food without the aid of modern methods and appliances.

1
FIREPLACE COOKING

In colonial times, stoves, ranges, microwaves, and convection ovens were not even imagined. Food was either boiled, roasted, fried, or baked in a fireplace. The fireplaces in the kitchens of the early settlers were so big that you and your family could have stood in them. But by the mid-1700s, smaller fireplaces were used because there was less wood.

Cooking on an Open Flame ⌣• The building of the fire in a colonial home took thought and planning. Every day at dawn, a large piece of wood was embedded in the ashes of a wide-mouthed fireplace. After the large wood was placed, a top log was added, then a fore stick, a middle stick, and a heap of kindling. All this was topped with a pyramid of smaller pieces placed with spaces for the blaze. Friction matches were not available to start the fire, so hot coals from the previous night or borrowed from a neighbor's fireplace were used. The last resort was to use flint, steel, and a tinderbox for striking a fire. This was a hard task, which took time and patience if the steel was soft and the tinder damp.

Cooking with an open fireplace was hot and dangerous. Many colonial women were killed when their long dresses caught on fire. Women often found it safer to hitch up their skirts and aprons and tuck them into their waistbands when cooking.

Another cause of burn injuries was the lug pole that was first used in fireplaces during the 1600s. This was a wooden bar placed across the fireplace for pots to hang from. This arrangement also required the cook to reach into the fire to remove a hanging pot and thus risk being singed. With time, the lug pole became charred and caused accidents when it suddenly broke apart.

In the early 1700s an improved bar made of iron, called a swing crane, came into use. It swung out from the fire so cooks could stir the ingredients or remove a pot without getting burned. Pots could also be raised and lowered with hook and chains to control the amount of heat they received from the fire.

Broiling or roasting was done by inserting a sharp iron rod, called a spit, through the middle of a joint of meat and supporting it in front of the fire with two forked uprights, called andirons or firedogs. A drip pan was placed underneath to catch the juices for gravy. In the first half of the 1700s, a small child was sometimes made to turn the spit so the meat would cook evenly. Another choice in some households was to use a stout dog, called a turnspit. The short-legged canine was trained to run on a wheel mounted on the wall above the fireplace. The wheel and spit were connected by a chain. As the wheel turned, so did the meat on the spit.

(9)

(10)

Fireplace cooking required the use of sturdy pots. Kettles and pots were the colonists' most expensive home furnishings. Brass, copper, and iron cookware were precious possessions. The most desired and loved of all these was the enormous iron pot, weighing about 40 pounds (18 kilograms) and holding up to 15 gallons (57 liters) of liquid. Besides being used to cook soups or stews, this vast pot was used for other chores, such as boiling laundry on wash day.

All the pots and kettles had long handles for hanging in the fireplace. Some also sat on trivets directly on the fire or stood on legs. One of these pots was called a spider because it was a three-legged black skillet, resembling the web spinner.

Baking ⌣ · Not everything was cooked directly on an open flame. Bread was cooked in an oven built into the chimney. On baking day, a fire was lit and allowed to burn until the bricks of the chimney were hot. After the ashes were swept, a cook would stick her arm up the chimney and into the oven. If she could count to ten, then the temperature was just right. Frequent bakers had no hair on their arms because it was singed off!

Food that needed to cook the longest, like baked beans, went into the oven first, then the bread and rolls. The oven was sealed with a heavy iron door and the food was left to cook until done. Often baking was planned for Saturday night supper so that the leftovers could be kept in the oven and eaten warm for Sunday meals. This custom developed from the colonists' religious beliefs. No work, including cooking, was permitted on the Sabbath (Sunday).

MAPLE WHEATEN BREAD
Makes 2 loaves

You will need:
1 package active dry yeast
1 cup warm water
3 tablespoons pure maple syrup, warmed
1½ cups white flour
1½ teaspoons salt
4 cups whole wheat flour

1 cup warm milk
2 tablespoons melted butter, plus extra for glazing

Equipment:
measuring cups and spoons
small and large bowls
fork
sifter

wooden spoon
floured board
large bowl, lightly buttered
dish towel
2 greased 8½-inch loaf pans
pastry brush
oven mitts
wire rack
knife for slicing

What to do:

1. Put yeast, ¼ cup warm water, and 1½ tablespoons maple syrup in small bowl.
2. Let soak for 1 minute, then mix with fork to dissolve yeast.
3. Sift white flour and salt into large bowl. Add whole wheat flour and stir to mix.
4. Make a well in the center of the flour, pour in yeast mixture, milk, butter, and the rest of the maple syrup and water. Slowly mix ingredients together with wooden spoon.
5. Mix until dough sticks together. Add more white flour if dough feels too soft and wet. Or add a little more water if dough will not come together.
6. Turn dough onto floured board and knead (work and press dough with the heels of your hands) until it is smooth and elastic, about 10 minutes.
7. Shape the dough into a ball. Put it in the lightly buttered bowl, rolling it over so ball is greased all over.
8. Cover with dish towel and let rise in a warm, draft-free place (about 80 degrees) until doubled in size, about 1½ hours.
9. Gently punch dough and fold sides into center. Knead again for 2 to 3 minutes.

10. Divide dough in half and shape into loaves, tucking the ends under.
11. Put into two loaf pans. Let rise again in warm place for 30 to 45 minutes.
12. Preheat oven to 400 degrees.
13. Brush loaves with melted butter, then place carefully in hot oven and bake for 30 to 35 minutes or until bread is well risen and browned.
14. Use oven mitts to remove pans and tip loaves out of their pans, tapping the bases of pans with blunt end of knife.
15. Place loaves on wire rack to cool. Slice and eat with butter.

How Did the Colonists Make Maple Wheaten Bread?

Ingredients: Dry yeast was not bought in packages at the store in colonial times. It was made at home from the froth that forms at the top of fermenting ale or beer. This yeast was called barm. It was mixed with flour and then covered with a linen cloth and blanket, kept warm overnight, and then added to the rest of the bread ingredients on baking day.

Equipment: Measuring was different in colonial days. There were no standard measuring cups and spoons. Recipes measured ingredients by weights. A colonial cook considered a good set of scales and weights an important piece of kitchen equipment.

A sandglass or the passage of the sun was used to tell the cook when the food was done, since there were no timers to set.

Another important kitchen tool used in bread making was a long-handled, flat wooden shovel, called a peel. It was used to slide the bread loaves (pans were not used) onto the hot bricks of the oven chimney and then to carry them out when they were done. This tool is still used by commercial bakers today to handle bread and pizzas.

2
PRESERVING AND STORING FOOD

Try to imagine a world without refrigerators. It would be impossible to eat fresh food all year long. Food transported over long distances from where it is raised to where it is eaten would spoil.

Preserving Foods ⌣· Fresh foods did not last long even if kept chilled. When the hunting was poor or the crops failed, starvation became a real danger. The colonists learned how to preserve food to make sure it was available in the long winter months.

The crowded colonial homes (some only had one room) lacked the storage space for a lot of preserved food. Thick-walled rooms, called root cellars, were dug under the homes to store food. Since the cellars were beneath the ground, they stayed cool and protected the food from the elements.

Drying was the easiest method of preserving food. The Native Americans taught the settlers how to make pemmican by drying venison in the sun, pounding it to shreds, and mixing it with melted fat, bone marrow, and wild berries.

Besides being mixed in pemmican, berries were often dried and eaten as we eat raisins today. Vegetables and fruit, such as green beans, corn, and apple slices were dried by stringing them together and hanging them up.

Pickling was also a popular method of preservation. Corn was made into corn relish, cucumbers into pickles, and many other foods were packed into a brine made of vinegar and salt. Honey was sometimes added to the vinegar to create a sweet-and-sour taste that is still a favorite with Americans. Meat and fish were kept from spoiling by being salted or smoked.

Fruits were made into thick preserves with the addition of honey or sugar. Cranberries were a particular favorite when candied and made into sauces. These deep-red berries grew wild in damp places, called bogs, along the New England coast. They were called *sassamanesh* by the American Indians and cranberries by the settlers because of the cranes that lived in the area. Cranberries were eaten raw or cooked. The sour taste didn't bother the colonists, but they enjoyed them more when sugar was added.

Keeping Things Cold ⤳• In colonial days there was no refrigeration. Only food found and grown close to home was eaten. To prevent perishable foods from spoiling too quickly, the colonists built sheds called springhouses, so named because they were built over flowing springs. The sheds kept animals away from the crocks of butter and jugs of cream that were put in the running water to stay cool.

In the southern colonies some wealthy settlers built insulated sheds called icehouses. During the winter, their slaves cut and carried large blocks of ice from frozen lakes and rivers. They loaded the blocks into the icehouses. Months after the end of winter, the icehouses kept food from spoiling while maintaining cool temperatures.

LEATHER BRITCHES

Leather Britches is the nickname the colonists used for dried stringbeans,
because they resembled men's pants hanging from a line.

You will need:
2 pounds fresh
  stringbeans
8 cups hot water

Equipment
kettle
adult helper
colander

1 large-eyed needle
fishing line

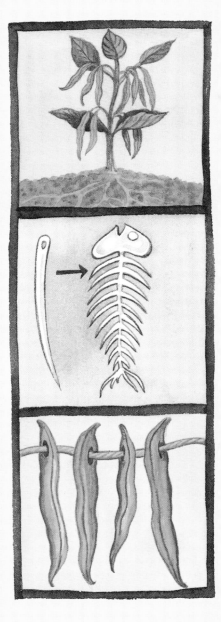

What to do:
1. Snip off the stems and tips of the beans with your fingers, then wash the beans.
2. Bring the water to a boil in the kettle. Add the beans and cook for one minute.
3. Have your adult helper drain the beans in the colander. Set them aside to cool.
4. Thread the needle with fishing line. String the beans by sewing through one end of each bean. Keep them from touching each other.
5. Hang the beans in a cool, dry place for about three days or until they feel crisp.
6. Store dried beans in plastic bags or sealed jars.
7. Before using beans in soups or stews, place them in a medium bowl and cover with boiling water. Let beans stand in water for about 2 hours to reconstitute (become plump).

How Did the Colonists Make Leather Britches?

Ingredients: Same

Kitchen equipment and method: Only wealthy colonists had steel sewing needles. Others might have used needles made of a cheaper metal or even of fish bones. Instead of fishing line, linen thread (made from flax) was used to hang beans from the kitchen rafters. The dried beans were cut down as needed for stews or soups. Boiling the water would have been done in a pot over the fireplace.

(17)

3
REGIONAL COOKING

The original thirteen colonies were divided into three regions: New England Colonies—New Hampshire, Massachusetts, Rhode Island, and Connecticut; Middle Colonies—New York, New Jersey, Pennsylvania, and Delaware; and Southern Colonies—North Carolina, South Carolina, Maryland, Georgia, and Virginia. Each region developed customs and food specialties, depending on its environment.

New England Colonies ⌁• New England's cuisine was plain and simple because of its rocky soil and short growing season. The easiest crops to grow were corn, squash, beans, and peas. Wheat did not grow well, so corn flour was used for most breads and puddings. Cranberries grew wild along the New England coast and were eaten when they ripened in the fall.

Pigs, which were native to the New England woods, were a source of pickled ham and salt pork for the colonists.

(18)

Fish were abundant in the eastern coastal waters of New England. Sometimes after a storm, 6-foot (1.8-meter) lobsters were washed onto the shore. Clams, crabs, and oysters were also plentiful.

By the 1700s, New Englanders started their own customs of eating. Before that time almost all the colonists had a breakfast of mush or pudding, similar to what they had eaten in England. Even though mush and puddings were still consumed in all the colonies, the New Englanders began a custom of eating cold meat, bread, milk, and fruit pies for breakfast. Apple pies were their favorite. In the winter they made stacks of pies and froze them in sheds. Each morning they set a frozen pie by the fireplace to defrost for breakfast.

The main meal of the day was eaten in the early afternoon. It was similar to what we would call dinner today. Fish chowders and bean dishes were popular for these big afternoon meals.

Dishes such as New England Clam Chowder and Boston Baked Beans began in colonial times and to this day are associated with the New England region.

One of the most popular customs in New England was eating salmon with peas and new potatoes on the Fourth of July. It was the time of the year when green peas and shiny potatoes were fresh from the garden and the salmon were running.

The Middle Colonies ⌣• There was more food variety in the Middle Colonies. Because of the milder climate and longer growing season, crops were easier to grow, including wheat, which could be made into finely grained breads and puddings.

Non-English settlers, such as the Dutch, had an influence on the cuisine in this region. Scrapple (mush made from pork scraps and cornmeal) and *oly koeks* (sweet dough fried in oil with raisins and bits of fruit) were favorites for breakfast in these colonies.

The colonists in the Middle Colonies loved sweets and ate an array of fancy cookies, pies, and many candied fruits with nuts and honey.

When the Shakers, a religious group, arrived in New York from England in 1774, a whole new way of cooking and healthy eating was established in the Middle Colonies.

The Shakers separated themselves from the "world" (people outside their religious group) and lived in communes (places where people shared the same beliefs, work, and possessions).

The Shakers had a strong belief in healthy eating. Their diet was varied enough to please the taste buds and the eye, while preventing indigestion and ailments. This religious order realized the value of eating more vegetables, fruits, and whole grains. They were also known for their cleanliness and creative uses of herbs. Besides cooking with herbs, the Shakers dried, ground, and packaged them to sell to the "world."

The Southern Colonies ⌣ • From the mid- to late 1700s the wealthier southern plantation owners had mountains of food at mealtimes. Their idea of a meal consisted of eight to nine courses. A typical breakfast included grilled fowl, prawns, ham and eggs, cornmeal mush, hominy, toast, cider, tea, coffee, and chocolate. All this was cooked and served by their slaves.

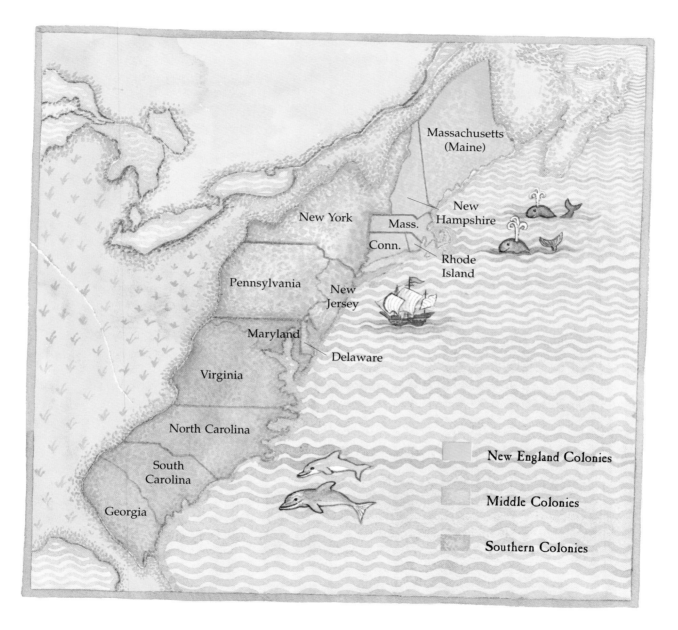

Massachusetts
(Maine)

New York

Mass.

New
Hampshire

Conn.

Rhode
Island

Pennsylvania

New
Jersey

Maryland

Delaware

Virginia

North Carolina

South
Carolina

Georgia

New England Colonies

Middle Colonies

Southern Colonies

(21)

The southern colonists who lived on smaller plantations or farms and owned only a few slaves, or none at all, did not eat so lavishly.

Beaten biscuits were very popular with all the southern colonists, but this hot bread probably would not have existed without the kitchen slaves. These biscuits required hard work and time to make.

Thomas Jefferson, author of the Declaration of Independence and the third president of the United States, was a gourmet (someone who enjoys food and is an expert on the art of cooking). His overseer said of Jefferson's eating habits, "He was never a great eater, but what he did eat he wanted to be very choice."

Thomas Jefferson brought home French and Italian recipes from his travels as a statesman in Europe. Some of his favorites were macaroni, Parmesan cheese, ice cream, and *pannequaiques* (crepes). He was often criticized by frugal John Adams for giving lavish dinner parties and serving so many "foreign" dishes instead of more traditional American food.

NEW ENGLAND CLAM CHOWDER
6–8 servings

You will need:
2 slices salt pork, chopped into small pieces
2 medium white onions, chopped
5 medium potatoes, cut into small cubes
2 10-ounce cans baby clams

⅓ cup butter
5 cups half-and-half (half milk and half cream)
2 teaspoons salt
½ teaspoon pepper

Equipment:
measuring cups and spoons
can opener and bowl
cutting board
paring knife
deep frying pan
wooden spoon

What to do:
1. Open cans and drain clams, saving juice.
2. Carefully fry salt pork in deep frying pan until lightly browned.
3. Stir in onion with wooden spoon and cook until soft but not brown.
4. Add clam juice from cans.
5. Add potatoes and cook until potatoes are tender, about 20 minutes.
6. Stir in butter, half-and-half, salt, pepper, and clams. Heat, but do not boil. Serve hot.

How Did the Colonists Make New England Clam Chowder?

Ingredients: In the 1600s and 1700s the colonists did not have the choice of using canned clams for this soup. Canned foods had not been invented yet. The New Englanders waited until the tide was out before walking through oozing sand to dig for clams. They then soaked the clams in a mixture of cold water, salt, and cornmeal for several hours. The clams had to be pried open and the muscles cut with a knife, after which the clam meat was boiled. The other ingredients were either in their springhouses or cellars.

Equipment: A more generous amount of this soup was cooked in the big pot the colonists had hanging in their fireplaces.

(23)

POTATO CAKES WITH ROSEMARY

Makes 12 pancakes

You will need:
3 large potatoes
1 egg
1½ tablespoons
  minced fresh rose-
  mary, or 2 teaspoons
  dried rosemary

salt and pepper
1 cup flour
vegetable oil for
  frying

Equipment:
vegetable peeler

knife
cooking pot to hold 3
  quarts of water
potato masher
mixing bowl
wooden spoon
10-inch heavy skillet
spatula

What to do:
1. Peel the potatoes and cut them in quarters.
2. Cook potatoes in pot of boiling water until tender. Have your adult helper drain the potatoes. Mash the potatoes.
3. Put mashed potatoes in bowl, add egg and beat with wooden spoon until blended.
4. Mix in rosemary. Season with salt and pepper.
5. Coat your hands with flour and divide potato mixture into twelve equal portions, then shape them into pancakes, flattening them with your floured hands. Each pancake should be about ½ inch thick. Continue to sprinkle hands with flour until all pancakes are coated.
6. Coat bottom of the heavy skillet with oil and heat over medium temperature. Add cakes and fry until they are lightly browned on both sides, about 3 to 4 minutes. Press them with the spatula to flatten them while frying.
7. Serve hot.

How Did the Colonists Make Potato Pancakes with Rosemary?

Ingredients: Butter would have been used instead of vegetable oil. Other herbs may also have been added to this recipe because the Shakers liked putting many herbs in one dish.

Equipment: A spoon was used to mash the potatoes. The pancakes were cooked in a skillet over hot coals.

BEATEN BISCUITS

Makes about 4 dozen biscuits

You will need:
8 cups unbleached
    flour
1 cup shortening
1 cup cold water
¼ teaspoon salt

½ teaspoon sugar

Equipment:
measuring cups and
    spoons
mixing bowl

fork
flat board
kitchen towel
clean hammer or
    mallet
2 cookie sheets

What to do:
1. Put flour in bowl with shortening, salt, and sugar. Mix with your hands until well blended.
2. Pour in water and mix well with fork until flour sticks together.
3. Place dough on flat board on strong table. Put a damp towel under board so it won't slip.
4. Pound dough with a hammer for about 20 minutes or until dough blisters and looks smooth and glossy.
5. Preheat oven to 400 degrees.
6. Pinch off piece of dough and form each piece into a ball about 2 inches in diameter. Place balls on cookie sheets and prick tops with the tines of a fork.
7. Bake biscuits for 20 minutes or until they are golden brown.
8. Serve hot with butter.

How Did the Colonists Make Beaten Biscuits?

Ingredients: Lard was used instead of shortening.

Equipment and method: To make biscuits the dough was placed on a chopping block or a tree stump and pounded with a hammer or the flat end of an ax. Southerners used to say three hundred whacks were enough, but for company no less than five hundred would do! All this pounding was to make the biscuits light and airy since there was no baking powder in colonial times.

4
HOT, COLD— EVEN NINE DAYS OLD

Soups! Tasty and hot! The colonists often enjoyed a delicious bowl of soup as they warmed themselves by their fireplaces. It was a meal they ate frequently because it was simple to make and freed women for other chores. They would put soup ingredients into the big iron pot that hung in the back of the fireplace and leave it to simmer for hours, even days.

Soups were made from anything on hand. Fresh vegetables were used in the spring and summer, dried ones in the winter. Venison, pork, fish, eel, turtle, squirrel, and even nuts were often added to the soup pot. If cream was available, generous amounts were poured into the soup mix. The colonists knew nothing about calories or cholesterol. The hard, physical work required to survive in the New World made for hearty appetites and lean bodies.

The settlers, especially the New Englanders, ate a lot of pumpkins and often put them in their soup pots. Nowadays we think of using pumpkins in desserts, such as pumpkin pies for Thanksgiving. But the colonists used them in many main dishes. They loved pumpkins so much that someone even wrote a poem about the orange squash:

We have pumpkins at morning
pumpkins at noon.
If it were not for pumpkins
we should be undoon.

—1630 anonymous poem

When fresh meat was available it was also thrown into the bubbling soups. Being cooked in soup made the meat soft and easy to chew. The colonists preferred it that way because many of them had trouble with their teeth. Fresh meat was rarely eaten in the form of roasts or steak because of loose teeth and toothaches. Not many dentists were around in colonial America. If home remedies for toothaches didn't work, often the local blacksmith extracted the teeth.

Soup was also useful when the colonials went on a journey. Since even the shortest distances took time to cover on foot, travelers filled their pockets with Portable Soup. This was made like any other soup, but no water was added to replace what boiled away during cooking. The soup was allowed to become thicker and thicker as it cooked over the fire. It was poured into dishes and was left to dry close to the fireplace. After several days, the soup dried out completely. It was then cut into little cakes and kept in a crock until the next trip was taken.

PUMPKIN SOUP
6–8 servings

You will need:
1 6-pound pumpkin
⅓ cup butter
1 tablespoon sugar
4 cups milk
2 teaspoons salt
½ teaspoon white
  pepper

Equipment:
large knife
cutting board
large soup pot
paring knife
pot holders
colander
electric blender

measuring cups and
  spoons
wooden spoon

What to do:
1. Wash pumpkin. Have an adult cut it into wedges, removing seeds and outer skin. Chop into smaller pieces.
2. Bring large pot of water to a boil. Add the pumpkin pieces and cook until tender when tested with a paring knife.
3. Drain in a colander.
4. Place some of the cooked pumpkin into blender. Mix in batches until smooth.
5. Put pureed pumpkin back in pot. Add butter and sugar, and cook over low heat for 15 minutes.
6. Use wooden spoon to stir in milk, a little at a time. Simmer for several minutes. Add salt and pepper. Serve hot.

How Did the Colonists Make Pumpkin Soup?

Ingredients: Maple syrup, honey, or molasses would have been used by the earliest settlers. White sugar was hard to get and expensive until the 1700s.

Equipment: Instead of a food blender, a sieve would have been used to puree the pumpkin. Scales were used instead of measuring cups and spoons. A large soup kettle was used to cook soup over the fire.

SPRING VEGETABLE AND HERB SOUP
6–8 servings

You will need:
2 medium leeks
3 medium zucchini
2 medium celery
  stalks
2 teaspoons fresh
  thyme leaves
1 cup fresh spinach
2 tablespoons butter

24 baby carrots
7 cups of vegetable
  broth
large strip of lemon
  peel
1 cup shelled fresh or
  frozen green peas
salt and pepper

Equipment:
cutting board
paring knife and
  larger knife for
  chopping
measuring cup and
  spoons
large kettle
wooden spoon

What to do:
1. Wash vegetables. Cut leeks into small pieces. Chop zucchini, celery, and thyme. Shred spinach with hands. Set aside.
2. Melt butter in soup kettle. Add carrots, leeks, and celery. Cover and cook over low heat for 10 minutes, stirring occasionally with wooden spoon.
3. Add broth, zucchini, lemon peel, and thyme. Bring to boil, then reduce heat and simmer until vegetables are tender, 20 to 30 minutes.
4. Add peas and spinach to soup. Season with salt and pepper. Simmer for additional 20 minutes. Take out lemon peel.
5. Serve hot.

How Did the Colonists Make Spring Vegetable and Herb Soup?

Ingredients: Spring and early summer were the only times fresh vegetables and herbs were available. Since there were no canned goods, fresh vegetable broth was added to the soup. To make the broth a variety of vegetables were sautéed in butter and then added to a pot of water. After the water was brought to a boil, the pot was moved farther away from the fire to simmer for several hours. The mixture was strained and the vegetables removed, leaving the broth clear.

Equipment: Large soup kettle to hang in fire, strainer, knives, large spoon for stirring.

This recipe made a good Portable Soup.

5
CORN: AN AGREEABLE GRAIN

Benjamin Franklin hungered for his beloved corn when he represented the colonies in London during the year of 1766. When the English commented that Indian corn in America was disagreeable, Benjamin Franklin defended the yellow vegetable in a letter to the London *Gazetteer*:

> Pray let me, an American, affirm that Indian corn, take it all in all, is one of the most agreeable and wholesome grains in the world…and that johnnycake or hoecake, hot from the fire, is better than a Yorkshire muffin…

When the first settlers came to America in the early 1600s, corn (called maize by the Native Americans) saved them from starvation. Since the American Indians were the ones who introduced this native crop to them, the colonists named it Indian corn. The American Indians grew several varieties of corn, not all of them yellow. Some were red, white, blue, and even black. Sweet corn was eaten as a vegetable and other types, like dent and flint, were ground into flour.

The colonists accepted corn as a way to become less dependent on the English. They had experienced hard times, waiting for delayed shipments of food and goods from England. They learned to adopt Indian ways of cooking and eating corn as well as other foods native to America.

The first time the colonists saw the American Indians eat corn on the cob, they were truly amazed. Never before had they seen a vegetable moved back and forth across the mouth in such a fashion.

The Indians also showed the colonists how to mix corn with meat and beans. This combination dish was called *succotash*. The oldest succotash recipe, from the early 1600s, described mixing boiled fowl with white beans, salt pork, turnips, potatoes, and cooked dried corn.

The early settlers in Virginia watched the American Indians make hominy (hulled dried corn) by using ashes and water to remove the skin from dried kernels. These hulled morsels were cooked as a soup mixed with meat and wild greens. Hominy was also ground coarsely and became known as grits (eaten as a cereal or a side dish) by southern cooks.

Popcorn ⌣• In addition to using Indian corn for tasty dishes, the Native Americans showed the settlers another variety of corn, called popcorn. As you know, this type of corn bursts into white, fluffy morsels when exposed to heat. The colonists had their first taste of this puffed corn when American Indians presented a deerskin bag of popcorn to the Pilgrims on the first Thanksgiving.

How do you think the Indians popped popcorn without butter, electricity, or cast-iron skillets? One of the methods they used was to insert a stick into the ear of popcorn and hold it over a campfire. Sometimes the kernels popped off the cob and went into the fire, the way we sometimes lose marshmallows in a campfire! Even though some popcorn was lost, the Indians liked this method best.

Other Indian ways for popping corn included throwing loose kernels into the fire. When the popcorn popped, it usually flew out of the fire and onto the ground. But this method required a lot of running about and bending. A third technique was the hot sand method. A layer of sand was put in a clay vessel and held over a fire. When the sand became very hot, the vessel was removed from the fire and kernels of popcorn were poured into the hot sand. The sand was stirred, and the popped kernels would rise to the top for easy removal.

The colonists were so impressed with popcorn that they served it at first as a breakfast cereal with sugar and cream. They worked on easier ways to pop the kernels and eventually designed a mesh shaker with a long handle. It was wearying work, standing by the fireplace and holding the shaker until all the kernels had popped.

Although corn was eaten in many enjoyable ways, most of the corn in colonial days was dried and ground into cornmeal. Cornmeal was either white or yellow, depending on the type of corn used. Even though the taste of both was basically the same, certain regions liked one color over the other. The southern colonies liked white cornmeal because of its pure color. The north, except for some areas in the New England region, was fond of the rich color of yellow cornmeal.

Cornmeal ᴗ· Because corn was easier to grow than wheat, the colonists used cornmeal more often than wheat flour for making bread.

The Native Americans taught the colonists how to grind the corn into cornmeal. Their method was to soak the corn kernels in hot water for twelve hours, then pound the grain in a mortar (hollowed stone or block of wood) until it was a coarse meal, called samp. It was then sifted in a woven basket. The pestle used to pound the samp was a heavy block of wood shaped like the inside of a mortar and fitted with a handle attached to one side. The pestle was attached to a young tree, bending a limb. The limb sprang up and down as the pestle pounded the corn. This primitive method was called the sweep-and-mortar mill.

By the mid-1600s, the colonists had built windmills to grind large amounts of corn. The American Indians were afraid of the windmills, thinking some evil spirit was turning the long arms and great teeth to bite into the corn.

Johnnycakes and hoecakes were both pancakes made of either yellow or white cornmeal. Johnnycakes were originally called Shawnee cakes by the Indians. They were also called "journey cakes," because colonial travelers would carry packages of them in their pockets.

Hasty Pudding, originally cooked in England with wheat flour, was made from cornmeal after the first settlers arrived in the New World. It was a favorite pudding in colonial times. Today we think of puddings as desserts, but in the 1700s puddings were more than just the last course of a meal. Most colonial households served pudding topped with milk and butter for breakfast and with gravy for supper. Sometimes pudding was the whole meal.

JOHNNYCAKES
Makes 12 cakes

You will need:
1 cup water
2 tablespoons butter
1 cup yellow cornmeal
½ teaspoon salt
½ teaspoon sugar

½ cup milk
Butter to grease skillet

Equipment:
measuring cups and
spoons

saucepan
mixing bowl
wooden spoon
skillet
spatula
platter

What to do:
1. Heat water and butter in saucepan until they boil.
2. Put cornmeal, salt, and sugar in mixing bowl while water and butter are boiling.
3. Pour boiling water and butter into mixing bowl. Add milk and stir with wooden spoon until batter is mixed.
4. Heat a pat of butter in the skillet over medium heat.
5. Drop six spoonfuls of batter into skillet. Cook for 3 to 4 minutes or until bubbles form on the surface of the cakes. Flip the cakes over with the spatula and cook other side.
6. Remove the cakes with spatula and place on platter. Keep warm.
7. Dab more butter on skillet and continue cooking rest of the Johnnycakes.
8. Serve immediately with maple syrup or apple butter.

How Did the Colonists Make Johnnycakes?

Ingredients: Honey and white cornmeal may have been used, depending on the time period and region.

Equipment and method: Johnnycakes and hoecakes were originally cooked on a hoe or a flat board over an outdoor fire by the Native Americans and early farmers. Corncakes were often packed for a long trip or carried out in the field when working. But in George Washington and Ben Franklin's day these cakes were cooked on a black iron griddle in the fireplace and eaten for breakfast with apple butter or maple syrup, if available.

(35)

HASTY PUDDING
6–8 servings

You will need:
4 cups milk
1 cup yellow cornmeal
butter to grease can
½ cup maple syrup

Equipment:
2-quart double boiler
measuring cups
wire whisk
wooden spoon

4-gallon cooking pot
2-pound coffee can
  with plastic lid
oven mitts
wire rack
deep bowl

What to do:
1. Fill the bottom pan of double boiler halfway up with water and bring to a boil.
2. Put the milk in the top part of the double boiler. Bring to a boil directly over medium heat.
3. Add the cornmeal into the boiling milk while mixing with the wire whisk to keep lumps from forming. Remove from heat.
4. Put top part of the double boiler over bottom part. Lower the heat. Add maple syrup to the cornmeal mixture and cook over simmering water, stirring often with the wooden spoon, for about 15 minutes. The cornmeal will look smooth and creamy.
5. Rub the inside of the coffee can with butter. When cornmeal is done cooking, pour it into the buttered mold (can).
6. Grease the inside of the can's plastic lid. If you don't have a lid, grease a piece of aluminum foil and fit it tightly over the can opening. Tie it with string.
7. Place can in large cooking pot filled with enough boiling water to come halfway up the side of the mold. Cover the pot. Cook over high heat until steam comes from the lid.
8. Lower the temperature. Cook for 2½ hours. Add more water if level lowers around can.
9. When done, remove mold carefully with oven mitts. Cool on rack while covered.
10. Uncover can and hold it upside down over a deep bowl. Tap the bottom of the can to remove pudding. Serve hot with butter and milk.

How Did the Colonists Make Hasty Pudding?

Ingredients: The first settlers made Hasty Pudding with just water and cornmeal. Then as times became more prosperous, milk, molasses or maple syrup, and sometimes eggs were added to the pudding.

Equipment and method: Instead of a wire whisk, the colonials used hand-made beaters like birch twig whisks. After the pudding was mixed, it was baked in a buttered pan or wrapped in a loose, floured sack and boiled for several hours. As the pudding steamed, the cornmeal swelled and filled the sack.

(37)

6
SOUL COOKING

The first African slaves arrived in America in the mid-1600s. Stuffed in their pockets were foods like peanuts, black-eyed peas, okra, and benne (sesame) seeds from their homeland in West Africa. They also brought with them a tolerance for hot spices like chili peppers and cayenne. These African foods and spices came to be combined with those that were native to the New World, such as corn, squash, beans, root vegetables, and greens.

The slaves created, out of necessity, a unique cuisine from these African and American flavors. This African-American cuisine remained nameless for more than two hundred years before it was called "soul food" for the first time in the 1960s.

Why was it called soul food? Soul food was eaten at the end of the day when the slaves were done with their work and had returned to their cabins. There they could be with their families, say prayers, sing, eat, and celebrate. They filled their souls as well as their stomachs.

Slavery was legal in all thirteen colonies by 1775. After the American Revolution, slavery began to disappear in the northern colonies because they had moved into manufacturing and trade. But the economy of the southern colonies continued to be based on crops such as tobacco, cotton, and rice, which needed many slaves to work in the fields.

Most slaves in the south lived on small or medium-sized farms. On these farms the master owned just a few slaves. But there were also some large rice plantations where many slaves lived.

Slaves on southern plantations and farms were often responsible for preparing their masters' meals. The kitchen building was separate from the main house to keep cooking smells and heat out of the house. When the food was ready, it was carried by slaves across a walkway between the kitchen building and the plantation house.

Except for the cooks, slaves were not allowed to eat the master's food. They were fed what was grown cheaply—peas, beans, sweet potatoes, rice, and cornmeal. If the slaves were permitted to grow a garden, after work hours, then they added fresh greens to their diet, such as turnip greens, mustard greens, dandelion greens, Swiss chard, collard greens, spinach, and kohlrabi. If given the time to fish, the slaves added catfish to their spicy stews, or fried mackerel and trout in cornmeal. Rarely was fresh meat given to them, except for pork.

After their masters took the best parts of the pig on butchering day—the ham, loin, and chops—the slaves were left with everything else but the squeal: head, snout, ear, jowl, neck, tongue, brains, hock, knuckles or feet, spareribs, stomach, stomach lining (hog maw), liver, tail, skin (cracklings), intestines (chitlins and sausage casings), and, best of all, bacon.

Besides greens and pork, the African slaves used benne seeds in many of their dishes. Benne seeds are also called sesame seeds, a name more familiar to us today. Many of the slaves believed that sprinkling their doorsteps with the seeds would bring good luck to the cabin and ward off ants. The most common uses of benne seeds were in stews, cookies, wafers, and biscuits.

The most reliable food in the diet of slaves was corn. Corn was made into all sorts of things, but a big favorite was hush puppies. These were deep-fried fritters made with cornmeal, buttermilk, flour, and onions. Traditionally, hush puppies were served with fried fish. Some say the name came from the kitchen slaves who used to throw fried cornmeal tidbits outside to barking dogs and shout, "Hush, puppies!"

Peanuts were another important part of the slaves' cuisine. When the Africans arrived in America, they continued to use peanuts as a vegetable (peanut butter sandwiches had not been invented yet).

Virginia farmers decided to grow the "slave food" (peanuts) and feed them to their pigs. So, whenever the slaves ran out of their treasured peanuts, they "borrowed" them from the pigs. One of the most delicious dishes the slaves made with these nuts was peanut soup. Today peanut soup is as famous in Virginia as bean soup is in Boston.

Black-eyed peas were yet another vital part of soul cooking. These peas are light brown with a small black dot on them.

A special dish called Hoppin' John was created in America by the slaves using black-eyed peas, rice, pepper, and bacon. It became a traditional food to welcome the new year. The slaves believed that if Hoppin' John was served before noon on New Year's Day, it would bring good fortune for the year ahead. There are different stories of how this dish got its name. One story was that a man named John came a-hoppin' when his wife made the dish. Another tale said children always hopped around the table before eating Hoppin' John.

As you have seen, the foods typical of most soul cooking were one-pot meals like soups, stews, and beans. Sweet potatoes were often included in these pots. But they were also roasted by themselves in the fireplace inside the slave cabins or outside during Saturday night gatherings at the slave quarters. Sweet potatoes were also made into desserts like hot sweet potato fried pies and puddings.

PEANUT SOUP

6 servings

You will need:
½ cup roasted peanuts
3 cups chicken broth
1 cup half-and-half
½ teaspoon chili
   powder

½ teaspoon salt
whipped cream

Equipment:
measuring cups and
   spoons

electric blender
medium saucepan
wooden spoon

What to do:
1. Blend peanuts with 1 cup of chicken broth in electric blender until smooth.
2. Pour into saucepan and add rest of chicken broth, half-and-half, chili powder, and salt. Stir with the wooden spoon.
3. Bring to boil, reduce heat and simmer slowly for 15 minutes.
4. Serve hot with a dab of whipped cream on top.

How Did the Slaves Make Peanut Soup?

Ingredients: The slaves would have roasted the peanuts themselves. The shelled nuts were placed in a skillet that was hung in the fireplace and raised or lowered to adjust the heat. The peanuts were turned in the skillet frequently to prevent scorching. Instead of chili powder, crushed red peppers may have been used.

Some slaves raised their own chickens and were permitted to sell the eggs. Occasionally a chicken was butchered and eaten by the slave family. The chicken broth would have come from the cooking liquid left from boiling one of these chickens.

Equipment and method: Instead of an electric blender to grind the peanuts, the slaves would have used a mortar and pestle. The soup ingredients were cooked in an iron pot hanging in the fireplace. The cream was whipped with twigs.

(42)

HOPPIN' JOHN
6 servings

You will need:

2 cups dried black-eyed peas
4 cups water
6 strips thick-sliced bacon
1 onion
1½ cups uncooked long-grain white rice
1 teaspoon salt
1 teaspoon black pepper

Equipment:
measuring cup and spoons
3-quart saucepan with lid
knife
cutting board
bowl
12-inch skillet
wooden spoon

What to do:

1. Put black-eyed peas and water in saucepan over high heat and bring to a boil. Reduce heat, cover pot with lid, and simmer peas until just barely tender—about 1 to 2 hours. Check the pot occasionally; you may have to add more water to keep peas covered.
2. While black-eyed peas are cooking, chop onion finely. Cut bacon slices into ½-inch pieces. Set aside.
3. Have an adult help drain cooked peas, saving the cooking liquid in bowl. Keep peas in the saucepan.
4. Sauté onion and bacon in skillet, stirring with the wooden spoon. When bacon pieces are golden brown and the onions are clear, add them to saucepan along with the fat in the skillet. Add the rice and 2½ cups of the peas' cooking liquid.
5. Add salt and pepper. Bring to a boil over high heat, then reduce heat and simmer covered, for 15 minutes.
6. Take saucepan off heat and let it stand with lid on for 10 minutes.
7. Spoon Hoppin' John into bowl and serve.

How Did the Slaves Make Hoppin' John?

Ingredients: Black-eyed peas were often planted in the slaves' gardens. In the summer the peas were picked and shelled early in the morning. They were cooked fresh or dried for winter meals. The rice was obtained from their masters and had to be washed by the slaves before using in dishes. Packaged rice today does not need to be washed.

Equipment: Iron skillets and pots were used to cook this simple dish over the fire.

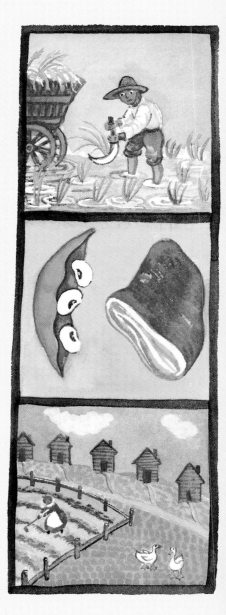

(43)

7

THINGS
TO DRINK

What would you think if your mother served you a glass of watered-down beer with breakfast one morning? Nowadays that would probably never happen, but in colonial days it did. Beer was the staple beverage for everyone from adults to infants when America was first settled in the early 1600s. The brew was so watered down, only about a ½ percent of alcohol was left in the drink—just enough to kill any bacteria in the water. The colonists feared waterborne diseases like cholera, typhoid, and dysentery, which they knew from their experiences in Europe. So when they arrived in the New World they were not in the habit of drinking plain water. Another reason they avoided water was that it was not easy to get. There were no sinks with running water in colonial homes, and in the winter the rivers and streams were often frozen.

The colonists first made beer from pumpkins, maple sugar, and persimmons. Later on, when barley and hops could be successfully grown in the colonies, beer was made from those ingredients, as it still is today.

Beer was the average person's drink, but wine was for the upper classes. Like the beer, the wine they drank was low in alcoholic content. The rich liked wine heavy and sweet. Unlike the beer, wines were imported. Thomas Jefferson tried to create an American wine industry, without success. There were two native grapes grown in America that were used locally: scuppernong (a plum-sized grape) and Concord grapes. But neither could compete in flavor with the imported wines.

Syllabub was a drink served at Christmastime. It was made "under the cow." A recipe, published in 1792 from Richard Brigg's *New Art of Cookery*, instructed the reader to hold a bowl filled with wine, lemon, sugar, egg whites, and nutmeg under a cow while she was being milked. The syllabub was ready when the liquid in the bowl had a nice froth to it. The recipe didn't say whether the cow was brought into the house or the guests went to the stable.

Other alcoholic drinks like those made with hard cider, brandy, rum, or whiskey, were given strange names like shrubs and bounces, The Bogus, Bombo, Rombo, Rumbullion, Rattleskull, Tiffs and Toddies, Stone Fences, and Whistle Belly Vengeance!

By the mid-1600s, the colonists cautiously began to drink water. There were times when they had nothing else to drink. They were pleased to find that instead of dying of a dreadful disease, their health improved. At this time milk also became a popular drink as the numbers of cows increased.

For most of the 1600s, the colonists had no tea, coffee, or chocolate to drink. They were unknown to the colonists because these beverages had not been introduced to England when America was first settled. But then in the early 1700s imports of tea came from East Indian companies. In the mid-1700s chocolate and coffee began to be shipped from South America.

The colonists used chocolate at first as an unsweetened drink, not a candy.

The settlers did not know how to consume tea and made some odd mistakes. Some boiled the tea leaves in water, threw the water out and ate the leaves. Others put butter and salt on the leaves. When they figured out the proper way to use tea, the colonists enjoyed it very much. By the time of the Stamp Act in 1765, when angry Americans threw taxed tea into Boston harbor, the colonists drank as much tea as the English.

To show support after the Stamp Act and during the Revolution, many colonists switched to drinking coffee instead of tea. They considered it a more patriotic drink. For some, it was hard to give up tea. For those who loved the hot beverage, another way to show patriotism was to make tea from raspberry leaves. This was called Liberty Tea.

The American colonists had their own tea etiquette and tea "signal": Turning the teacup upside down on its saucer and placing the spoon on top meant you wished no more tea. One story was told about a visiting Frenchman who knew nothing about the signal and became desperate when served his sixth cup of tea. He finally stuffed the teacup into his pocket after emptying it.

LIBERTY TEA
Makes 6 cups

You will need:
6 cups water
3 teaspoons dried
  raspberry leaves
  (available at health
  food stores)
honey to taste

Equipment:
measuring cup and
  spoons
saucepan or tea kettle
strainer
teapot and pot holder

6 teacups and
6 teaspoons

What to do:
1. Pour 6 cups of cold water into a tea kettle or saucepan. Heat on high until it boils.
2. Put the raspberry leaves into the teapot.
3. Have an adult pour boiling water into the teapot. Let tea steep (brew) for 5 minutes.
4. Pour the tea through the strainer into teacups. Sweeten tea with honey.

How Did the Colonists Make Raspberry Tea?

Ingredients: Raspberry leaves were picked off the berry stems and rinsed lightly with cold water. Usually the leaves were dried inside the colonial home by the fireplace. They were placed on a flat tray set on blocks of wood. The leaves were turned every day so they would dry evenly.

Equipment: The kettle for boiling the water was hung in the fireplace. Teapots were usually made of pottery or pewter. Some of the teacups had no handles and were called teabowls.

(47)

8

FEEDING THE SWEET TOOTH

In early America there were no candy bars, packaged cupcakes, or boxed cookies sitting on a store shelf for people to buy. In the 1600s, desserts as we know them were rarely made because sugar and molasses, both imported from the West Indies, were far too expensive. The only sweetener the first settlers had ever used in their food was honey. But when the Native Americans introduced maple sugar to the colonists, a whole new set of sweet dishes were added to the colonial diet.

Maple Sugar ⌣· Maple sugar was the only flavoring that Indians in the American northeast used in their food. They put it on everything from popcorn to meat and boiled fish. They called it their forest sugar.

Under the "maple moon," the American Indians tapped the precious maple trees they called *sheesheegummawis* (meaning "sap flows fast"). The sap, a watery liquid, was placed in a pot made of bark. Hot rocks were then dropped into the sap to cook it down to sugar. It turned into a thick syrup deep brown in color and sticky with insects, twigs, and pieces of bark. Even so, the American Indians loved this sugar because it helped them feel full when the hunting was not good and meals were skimpy.

This sugar-making time was a big festival for the American Indians. They held ceremonial dances, and mothers made *mokuks* (birch-bark boxes) to fill with the first sugar for their children.

One interesting way the American Indians stored maple syrup was to make "wax sugar."

The New England colonists loved maple sugar and learned to store it in wooden tubs for use the whole year. They put it in pies, puddings, jam and preserves, pickles, cornmeal mush, cured meats, and used it for sweetening their coffee and tea. Maple sugar became a valuable staple.

The colonists wanted to protect the maple trees and keep them alive from year to year. The Indians used hatchets to gash the maple trees to collect their sap, and often the trees died afterward. So the colonials learned to bore a hole in the maple tree to drain the sap. When the sap was removed, a plug made of wood from the same tree was put into the hole. The maple trees survived this method and could then be tapped again and again.

White Sugar ⌣• In the beginning of the 1700s the cost of white sugar went down, and the not-so-wealthy colonists were able to purchase it. This fine sugar then became more commonly used than either honey or maple sugar because it was easier to acquire and store. Unlike the granulated sugar we use now, white sugar in the 1700s was pressed into a cone shape and packaged in blue paper. Colonial cooks pinched chunks of sugar from the cones with sugar nippers (small tongs).

Along with the use of sugar came the introduction of ice cream. Thomas Jefferson wrote down the first ice-cream recipe in America and George Washington had the first ice-cream maker on record. Thomas Jefferson liked to experiment with different ice-cream dishes and was fond of serving ice-cream balls enclosed in cases of warm pastry. Guests were astonished when the ice cream survived the heat and remained unmelted.

Besides sweetening their tea and coffee with sugar, the colonists loved sweetened cakes with their hot drinks. Not everyone could have these sweets daily, but wealthy colonists like George Washington's wife, Martha, served sweets often at the dinners given at Mount Vernon. Her recipe for Great Cake used forty eggs with lots of sugar, flour, candied citrus, and cherries. This sweet cake weighed about 11 pounds (5 kilograms) and was served at Christmastime. Other cakes were less elaborate and cheaper to make. They were a favorite with many colonists for special occasions.

Adding sugar to fruit in season was a simple way for the colonists to eat dessert. The first settlers found fruits like strawberries growing wild in the meadows. They wrote home, "The strawberries are four times bigger and better than ours in England."

Flummery was another dessert made with fruit that was served at the end of many elegant dinners. Each region in the colonies developed their own types of desserts. But it was the New England cooks who became best known for the whimsical names they gave to their cookies and other baked goods: Jolly Boys, Tangle Breeches, Kinkawoodles, and Snickerdoodles.

(51)

WAX SUGAR
6–8 pieces

You will need:
1 pint real maple
  syrup
6 trays of ice cubes

Equipment:
saucepan
candy thermometer
snow-cone maker,
  food processor, or
  kitchen towel and
  hammer

cookie sheet
ladle
wooden spoon
pot holder

What to do:
1. Put syrup in saucepan and bring to a slow boil over medium heat.
2. Keep cooking the syrup until the candy thermometer reaches 235 degrees. This is the soft-ball stage.
3. While the maple syrup is cooking, crush ice cubes in snow-cone maker or food processor, or wrap them in kitchen towel and hit with hammer.
4. Put the crushed ice in an even layer on the cookie sheet.
5. Using the pot holder, tilt saucepan over the cookie sheet. Use ladle to drizzle syrup over the ice.
6. Let the syrup cool and then peel the candy off the crushed ice and eat like taffy.

How Did the American Indians Make Wax Sugar?

Ingredients: Snow on the ground was used, not ice cubes.

Equipment and method: The American Indians had no candy thermometers to judge the readiness of the maple syrup. They learned to watch the color and thickness of the cooking syrup to know when it was ready. They drizzled the hot syrup on the snow and waited for it to cool. Then the American Indians peeled off the taffy and packed it away for journeys.

(52)

BLUEBERRY FLUMMERY

6 servings

You will need:
3 cups fresh blueberries
¾ cup cold water
1 cup white sugar
½ teaspoon salt
6 tablespoons corn-
starch

Equipment:
measuring cups and
spoons
colander
3-quart saucepan with
lid
wooden spoon

small bowl
fork
pot holder
6 small dessert cups or
6-cup jelly mold

What to do:
1. Put blueberries into colander and run cold water over them.
2. Put the water and blueberries in saucepan. Cover saucepan and cook berries over medium heat for about 10 minutes, or until they are soft. Stir them a few times with the wooden spoon while they cook.
3. While the berries cook, measure the sugar, salt, and cornstarch into bowl and stir with fork.
4. Slowly add the sugar mixture to cooked berries and stir. Turn down the heat and simmer mixture for another 10 minutes, or until it becomes thick.
5. Spoon the flummery into dessert cups or jelly mold. Chill before serving. To serve from a jelly mold: Dip a small pointed knife in warm water and slide it around the rim to loosen the top edge. Place a large plate upside down on top of the mold. Hold the plate and mold together and quickly turn them over. Tap lightly on the bottom of the mold until the chilled flummery slides out.

How Did the Colonists Make Blueberry Flummery?

Ingredients: Other berries, such as raspberries, were also used in this recipe. Since cornstarch was not available as a thickener, a clear gelatin was made from the great bones in a calf's foot. The bones were cut out of the foot and boiled in water, then strained, making a clear jelly to use in this recipe.

Equipment and method: Colonial cooks liked shaping flummery in jelly molds. It was then spooned into glass dishes before serving at the end of a fine dinner. The molds would have been chilled in an icehouse in the south and in a springhouse in the other colonies.

(53)

9
MANNERLY EATING

A book on colonial foods would not be complete without some comment on the way in which the foods were served.

In the 1600s and early 1700s, only on Sundays did the early colonial families sit down and have a meal together. They were far too busy the rest of the time. During a typical day a hungry parent or child would hurry in and grab a quick bowl of soup or stew from the big pot hanging in the fireplace. Most of the time they ate standing up before rushing off to do more chores.

Everyone had tables in their homes even though they did not always sit at them. Most were not tables at all, but boards without legs set on supports resembling sawhorses.

Seating was different, too. There were never enough chairs or stools for everyone. A long narrow bench without a back, called a form, was placed on each side of the board. In some colonial households children were never allowed to sit, even on these forms, during meals. They had to stand by the side of the board for the entire meal as food was handed back to them by a parent or another adult.

In the households where the children were allowed to sit at the table, a list of rules for their behavior had to be followed. Some rules from a book printed at the time of the Revolution called *A Pretty Little Pocket Book*, says that children were:

1. Never to seat themselves at the table until after the blessing had been asked.
2. To wait for their parents to tell them to sit.
3. Never to ask for anything on the table.
4. Never to speak unless spoken to.
5. Always to break bread, never bite into a whole slice.
6. Never to take salt except with a clean knife.
7. Look not earnestly at another person that is eating.
8. Throw not bones under the table.

In the 1600s and early 1700s, dozens of cloth napkins were used during meals. The colonists needed them because forks were not known to the average person and most solid food was eaten with the hands. The only eating utensils were cups, spoons, knives, and trenchers used as plates. Chafing dishes were used to serve hot food, and in the middle of the board sat a salt cellar (an open container holding salt). All the eating utensils were made of pewter, silver, wood, or leather.

Throughout the period, trenchers were used as plates. They were square blocks of wood with bowls hollowed out on one side. The food was placed in these hollows. Colonial families never had enough trenchers for everyone. Usually a husband and wife ate from one and the children from another. Most people did not have their own drinking cups. A common cup was passed around the table, and everyone drank from it. In colonial times no one knew anything about germs.

China plates were not used until the time of the Revolution in 1776. East Indian trade opened up, and large cargoes of Chinese pottery and porcelain enabled all but the poorest families to own china dinner plates.

In the late 1700s, as colonists prospered in the New World, table manners grew more refined. George Washington said it all when he quoted a rule from a book of manners, "Cleanse not your teeth with the tablecloth, napkins, fork, or knife."

At this time, wealthy families had separate dining rooms added to their homes and real tables built. The use of forks, spoons, plates, and glassware became popular with wealthy and middle-class colonists.

The next time you sit down with your family to eat a meal, think about your colonial heritage and how food and eating customs have changed in the last three hundred years.

APPENDIX

Additional directions for using recipes in a classroom with your teacher and classmates:

Chapter 1
Maple Wheaten Bread: Extra equipment needed: portable toaster oven.

Chapter 2
Leather Britches: Extra equipment needed: portable electric burner to boil water.

Chapter 3
New England Clam Chowder: Extra equipment needed: 2 electric frying pans, another wooden spoon.
Increase ingredients: Double recipe.

Potato Cakes with Rosemary: Extra equipment needed: electric skillet.
Increase ingredients: Double recipe and make potato cakes smaller.

Beaten Biscuits: Extra equipment needed: portable toaster oven.

Chapter 4
Pumpkin Soup: Extra equipment needed: Use two Crock-Pots instead of one large soup pot.
Increase ingredients: Double recipe; make one recipe in each Crock-Pot. Allow for extra cooking time.

Spring Vegetable and Herb Soup: Extra equipment needed: One Crock-Pot instead of kettle. (Two Crock-Pots for class of over 30 students.)
Increase ingredients: For large class, double recipe—one recipe for each Crock-Pot. Allow extra cooking time.

Chapter 5
Johnnycakes: Extra equipment needed: Use two electric skillets, a portable electric burner, and one more spatula.
Increase ingredients: Double recipe.

Hasty Pudding: Extra equipment needed: Portable electric burner, another 2-pound coffee can.
Increase ingredients: Double recipe. Place two cans in large pot instead of one.

Chapter 6
Peanut Soup: Extra equipment needed: Two Crock-Pots instead of one pot.
Increase ingredients: Double recipe—one recipe in each Crock-Pot. Allow for extra cooking time.

Hoppin' John: Extra equipment needed: Portable electric burner, another saucepan, one electric skillet.
Increase ingredients: Double recipe.

Chapter 7
Liberty Tea: Extra equipment needed: Portable electric burner, another teapot.
Increase ingredients: Double recipe.

Chapter 8
Wax Sugar: Extra equipment needed: One more candy thermometer, portable electric burner, saucepan, wooden spoon, ladle, pot holder, and cookie sheet.
Increase ingredients: Double recipe. One pint of maple syrup in each saucepan. Increase ice cubes.

Blueberry Flummery: Extra equipment needed: Portable electric burner. Another saucepan, wooden spoon, pot holder, small bowl and fork, second jelly mold (if using).
Increase ingredients: Double recipe.

BIBLIOGRAPHY

Addy's Cookbook. Middleton, Wisconsin: Pleasant Company Publications, Inc., 1994.

Belote, Julianne. *The Compleat American Housewife 1776.* Concord, California: Nitty Gritty Productions, 1974.

Blanchard, Marjorie Page. *Treasured Recipes from Early New England Kitchens.* Charlotte, Vermont: Garden Way Publishing, 1978.

Blassingame, John W. *The Slave Community.* New York: Oxford University Press, 1972.

Borreson, Mary Jo. *Let's Go to Mt. Vernon.* New York: G. P. Putnam's Sons, 1962.

Delong, Deanna. *How to Dry Foods.* Tucson: HP Books, 1979.

Earle, Alice Morse. *Home Life in Colonial Days.* New York: The Macmillan Company, 1898.

Editors of *American Heritage, the Magazine of History. The American Heritage Cookbook. Part 1 and Part 2.* New York: American Heritage Publishing Co., 1964.

Evitts, William J. *Captive Bodies, Free Spirits: The Story of Southern Slavery.* New York: Julian Messner, 1985.

Felicity's Cookbook. Middleton, Wisconsin: Pleasant Company Publications, Inc., 1994.

Fritz, Jean. *George Washington's Breakfast.* New York: Coward-McCann, Inc., 1969.

Frost, Heloise. *Early American Recipes*. Newton, Massachusetts: Phillips Publishers, Inc., 1953.

Gemming, Elizabeth. *Maple Harvest*. New York: Coward, McCann and Geohegan, Inc., 1976.

Harrison, Molly. *The Kitchen in History*. New York: Charles Scribner's Sons, 1972.

Ingraham, Leonard W. *Slavery in the United States*. New York: Franklin Watts, Inc., 1968.

Jones, Evan. *American Food: The Gastronomic Story*. New York: E. P. Dutton & Co., 1975.

Kimball, Marie. *Thomas Jefferson's Cook Book*. Richmond: Garrett Massie Publishers, 1949.

Leonard, Jonathan Norton, and the Editors of Time-Life Books. *American Cooking: New England*. New York: Time-Life Books, 1970.

Lizon, Karen Helene. *Colonial American Holidays and Entertainment*. New York: Franklin Watts, Inc., 1993.

MacMillian, Norma. *In a Shaker Kitchen*. New York: Simon & Schuster, 1995.

Penner, Lucille Recht. *The Colonial Cookbook*. New York: Hastings House, 1976.

———. *The Honey Book*. New York: Hastings House, 1980.

Phillips, Ulrich B. *American Negro Slavery*. Baton Rouge: Louisiana State University Press, 1966.

Sloane, Eric. *ABC Book of Early Americana*. New York: Henry Holt and Co., 1963.

Smith, Jeff. *The Frugal Gourmet Cooks American*. New York: William Morrow and Co., 1987.

Taylor, Dale. *The Writer's Guide to Everyday Life in Colonial America*. Cincinnati: Writer's Digest Books, 1997.

Thurber, Nancy, and Mead, Gretchen. *Keeping the Harvest: Home Storage of Vegetables and Fruits*. Charlotte, Vermont: Garden Way Publishing, 1976.

Trager, James. *The Food Chronology*. New York: Henry Holt and Co., 1995.

Train, Arthur Jr. *The Story of Everyday Things*. New York and London: Harper and Brothers Publishers, 1941.

Tunis, Edwin. *Colonial Living*. New York: Thomas Y. Crowell Co., 1957.

Walter, Eugene, and the Editors of Time-Life Books. *American Cooking: Southern Style*. New York: Time-Life Books, 1971.

Warner, John F. *Colonial American Home Life*. New York: Franklin Watts, Inc., 1993.

Williams, Barbara. *Cornzapoppin'!* New York: Holt, Rinehart and Winston, 1976.

INDEX

ABOUT THE AUTHOR AND ILLUSTRATOR

This is a first book for **Loretta Frances Ichord**, although she has another under way. An active member of the Society of Children's Book Writers and Illustrators, she was able to combine her passion for cooking and her joy of traveling to historic sites into a book project. Ms. Ichord is the mother of four grown children and lives in Hickman, California.

Jan Davey Ellis has illustrated many successful books, among them *The Quilt Block History of Pioneer Days With Projects Kids Can Make* by Mary Cobb, *Winter Solstice* by Ellen Jackson, and *Toad Overload* by Patricia Seibert. When she is not working on children's books, Ms. Ellis designs wall murals and painted furniture.